The Odd Cod

By RL Lane

So many odd things happened on our trip to the cape that the title had to reflect it...

It started with the memory of him as a little boy. Putting the towel over his shoulders and tying it to make a cape. My brother.

Why can it not be that easy? Take a towel from the closet and don it on our shoulders to become whatever we wanted. I have a lot of towels. I could be a different person every day...

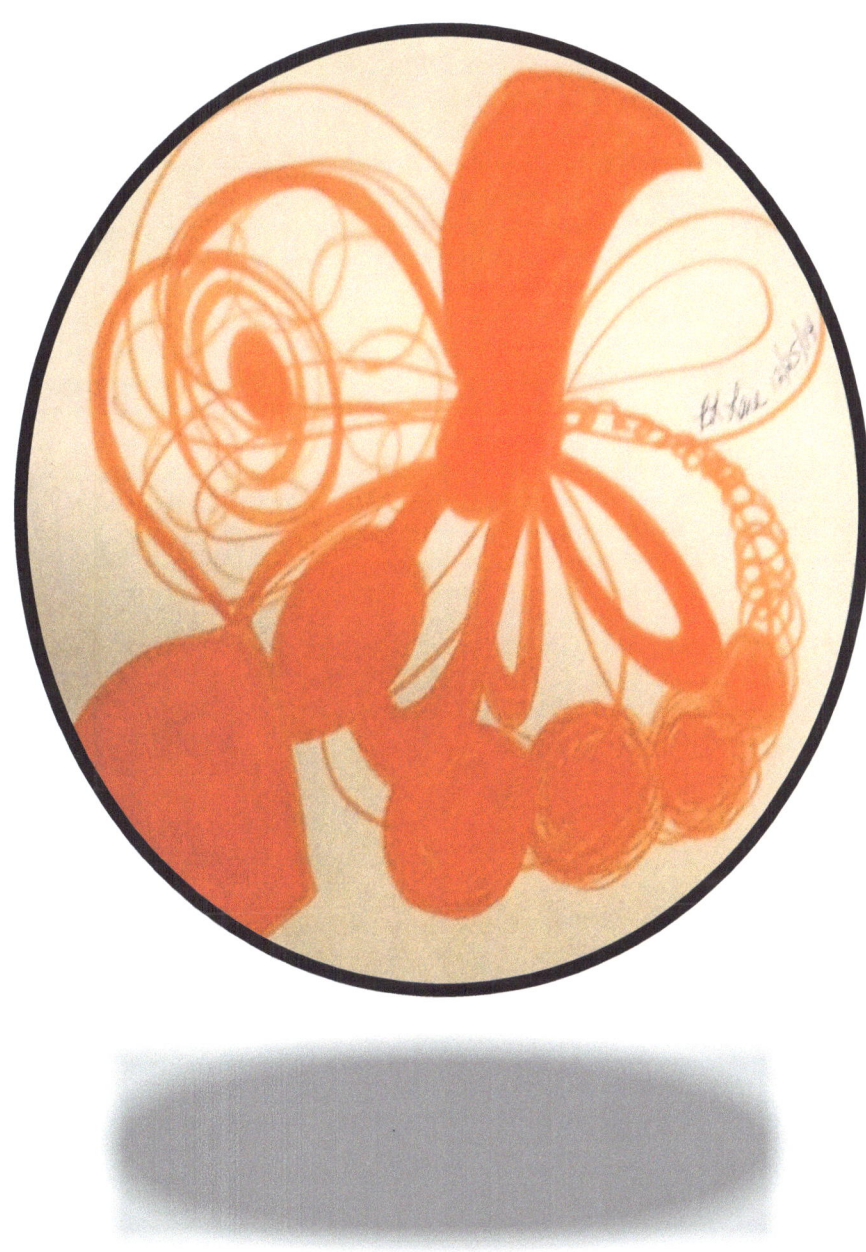

If I was a different person every day…who would I be?

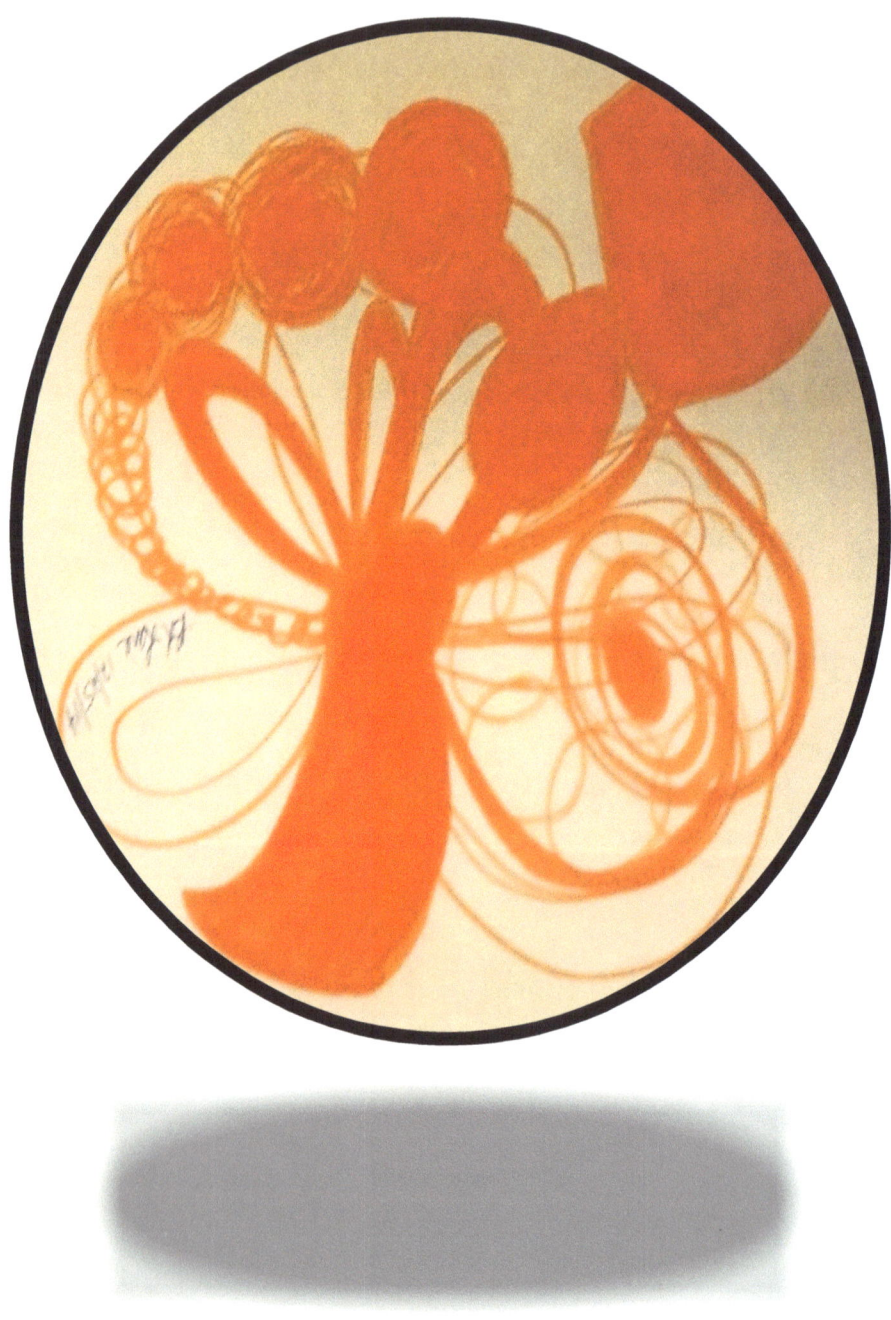

On the way to the cape we passed through one of the larger Connecticut or Rhode Island cities. I am not sure which. It was already getting dark. There were tall buildings with hundreds of empty offices. The night lights were on so we could easily see inside. The still and quiet offices. I kept looking at them. It made me wonder about all the daytime activities that would be going on when the work day began again. The people and their motions. Getting up from their desks to go to the break room or to the copier or to the fax. On their phones. Typing on their computers. Talking to their co-workers…

It was pitch black by the time we actually crossed the Massachusetts border. At one point, driving along, I was overcome by peace. Pitch black. Nothing to see, yet I already knew I would like it there. I could feel it in the air…

Chatham. We arrived around 1:30 in the morning…

I was only dropping off my daughter. She was staying with a college friend and her family. They let me stay the night because it was such a long trip. It makes me happy to know that my daughter already has so many people in her young life who are genuinely caring and loving people.

I had a dream that first night of a woman with blond curly hair. Tight curls. Close to her head. She was middle age. She was being protective of her man. I don't know what this message is…

I stayed the next morning to do a few drawings before returning to NJ. I walked down a path through tall grass to get to some picnic tables. Dodging the ticks just waiting to attack…

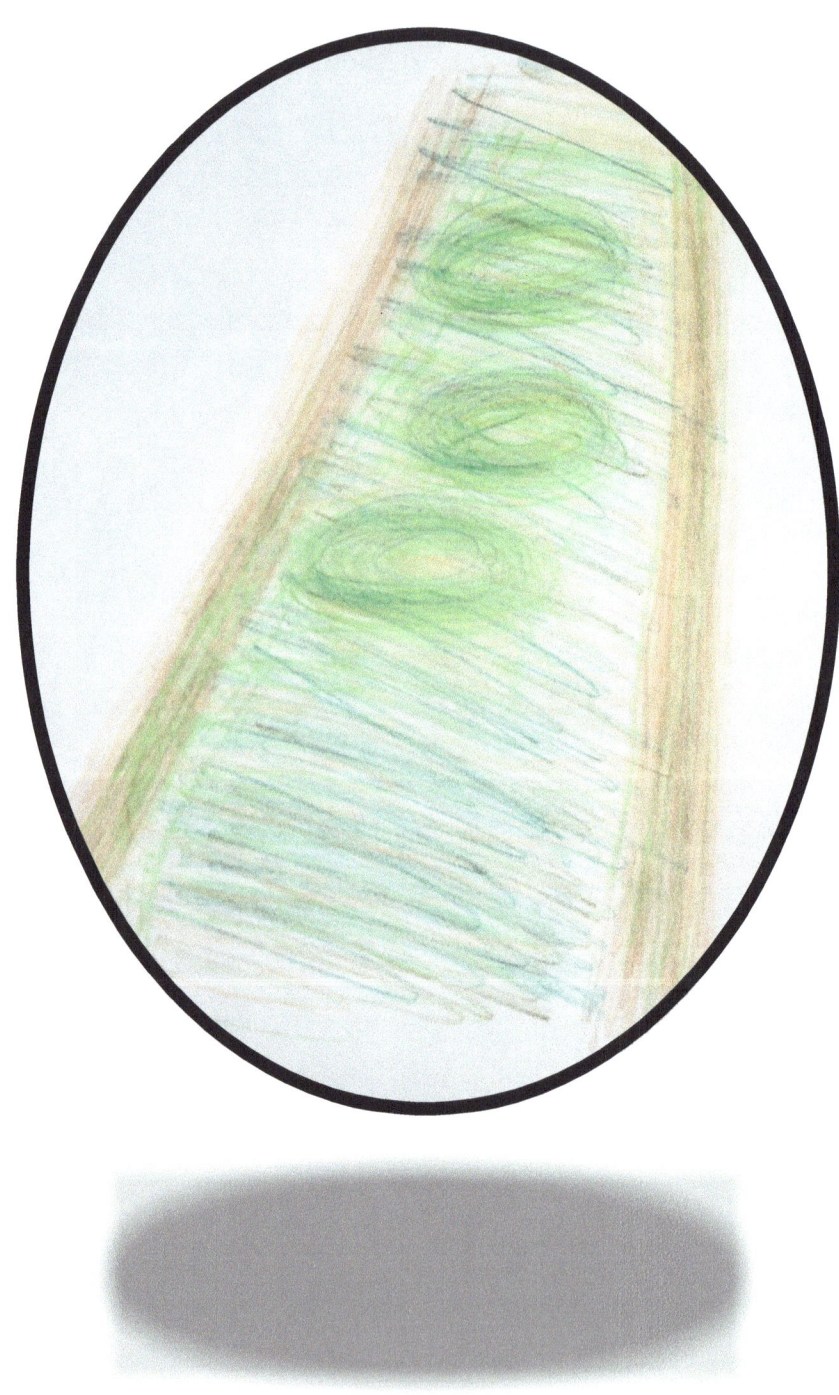

I sat down to draw. The water was in front of me. The first picture I drew was of the rock splashing in the water…

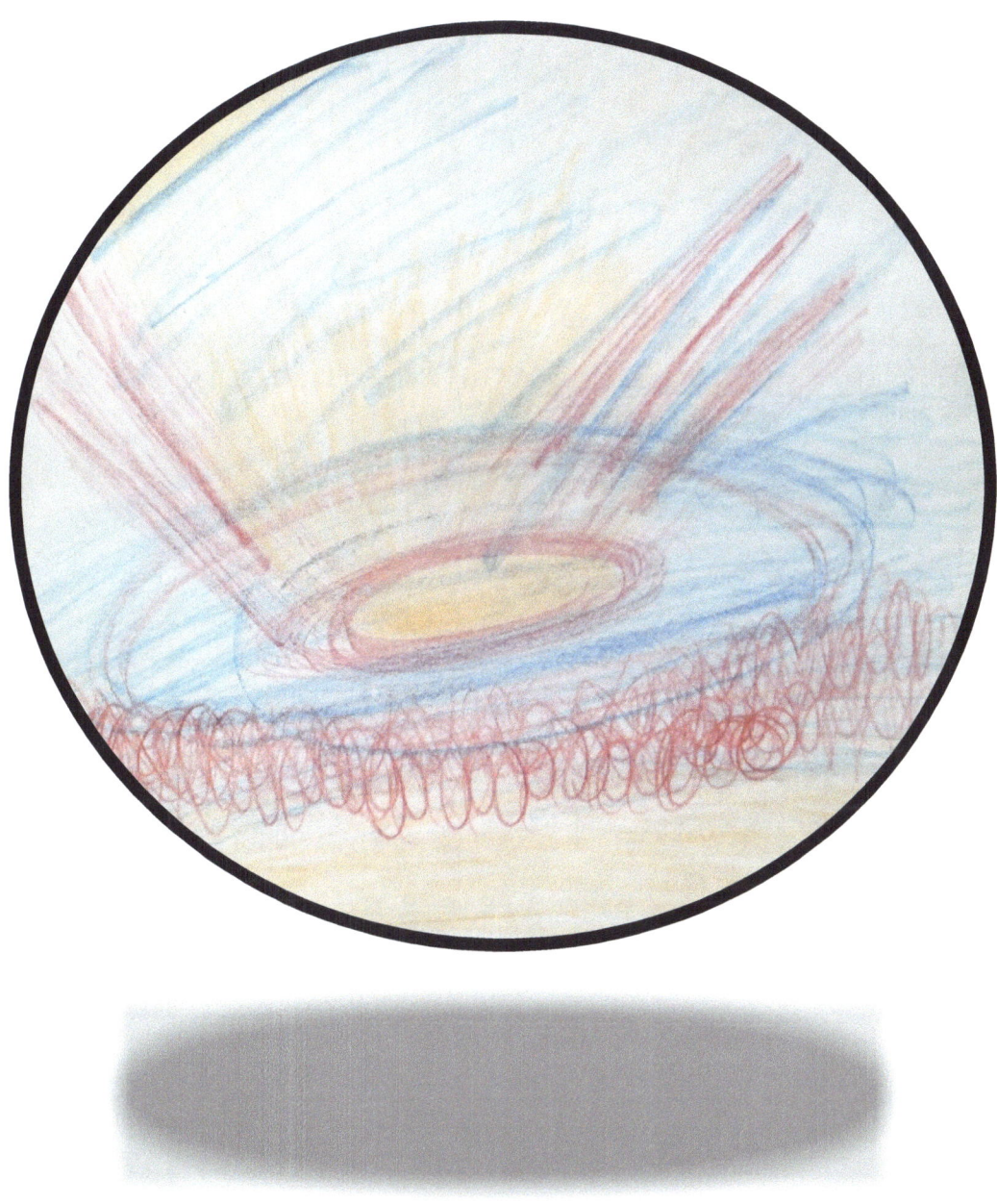

Reminded me of throwing the rocks into the upstate NY lakes. Them skipping across the water. How many skips could you make it do? Oh the skipping. With the rope.

Around and around

over my head

and under my feet.

Up and down.

I was a good skipper. Oh. The skipper. I would probably not be a good skipper of a ship if we were lost on a deserted island. It brought me back to the house where my daughter was staying. It is not on a deserted island, but it feels pretty secluded. Neighbors yet still able to have privacy. I drew a neighboring house. It had the flags out in front…

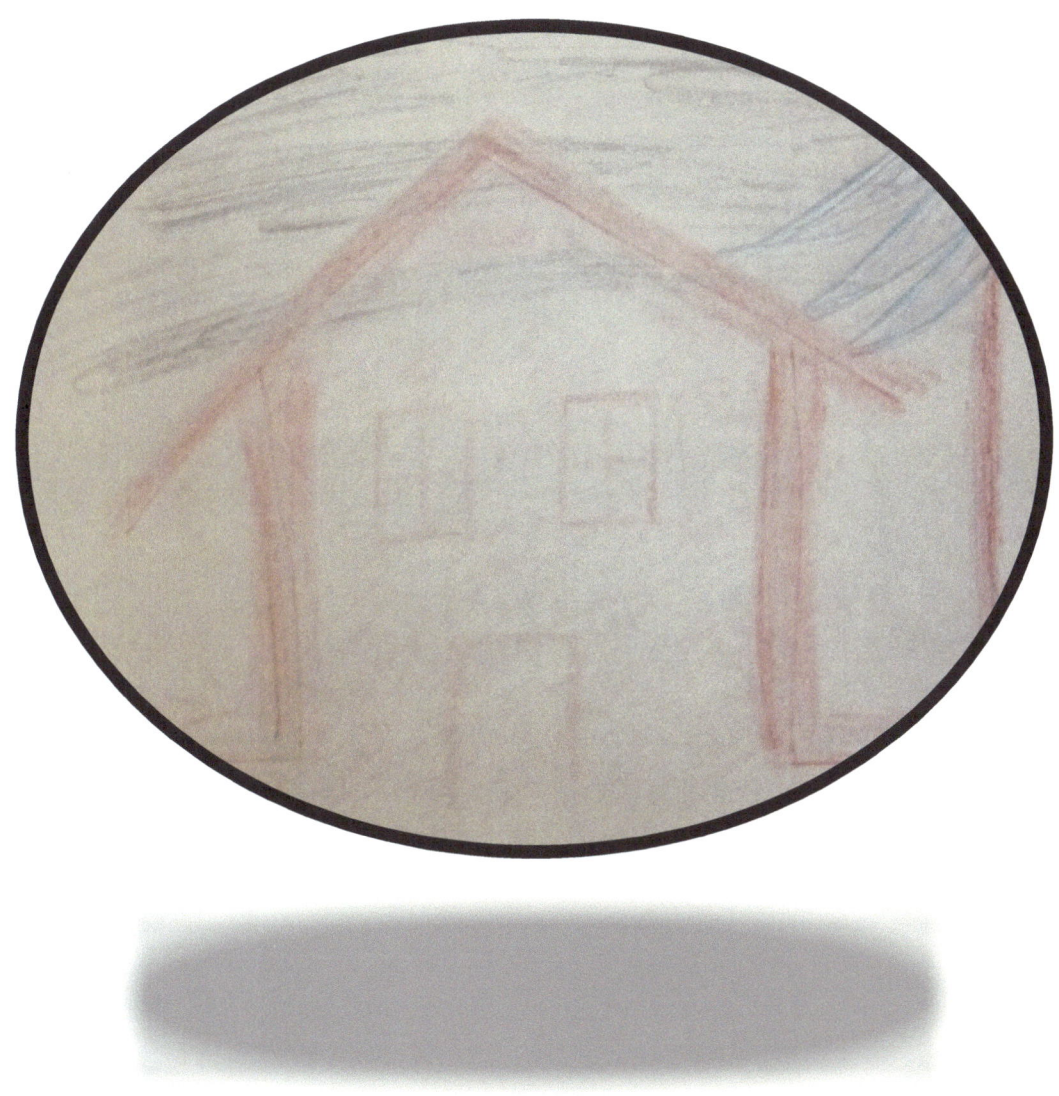

Just blowing that day in the breeze. Partly sunny. Partly cloudy. It didn't matter. *The weather could not take away the moments of the day…*

When we had first arrived, my daughter walked in and stopped partway. She turned around and commented that it reminded her of the Bratingham Lake camp of her childhood with her cousins. Upstate NY. I was glad that memory is a pleasant one. I remembered the dream again. The house was full of people…full of life…love and laughter. A large family reconnecting, resting, sharing, living…

The friend she was staying with had her own fond memories of childhood summers in that house. She said something about the ducks in the house…ducks are on the lake she says…we are not on the lake…why are there ducks…

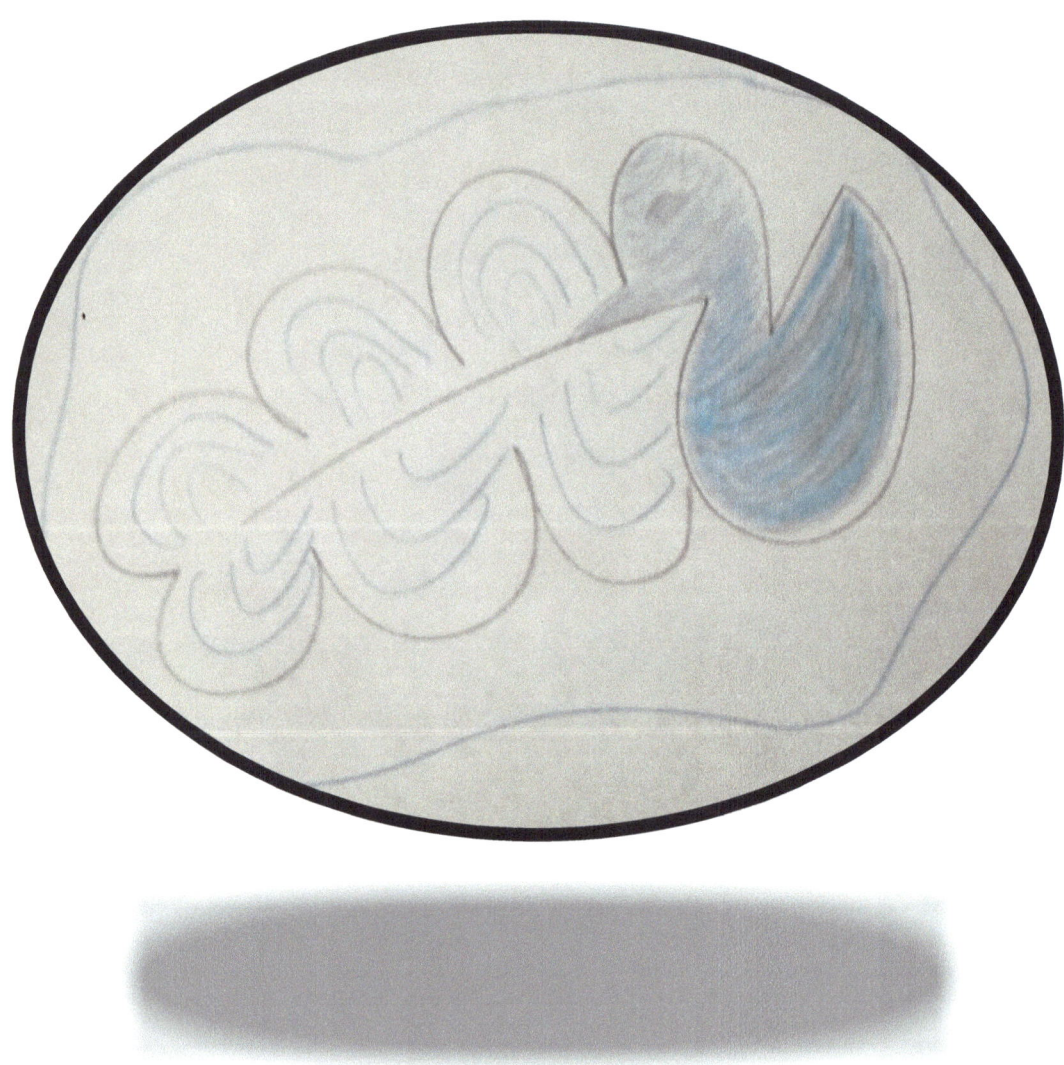

The next drawing was odd. It was easy to see it was the crossroads. But why were they all leading to the water? I am supposed to move to the city in a few months. There is no clear blue water there. What does this mean? Perhaps this is something for the future. It does feel like I am at a crossroads in my life…

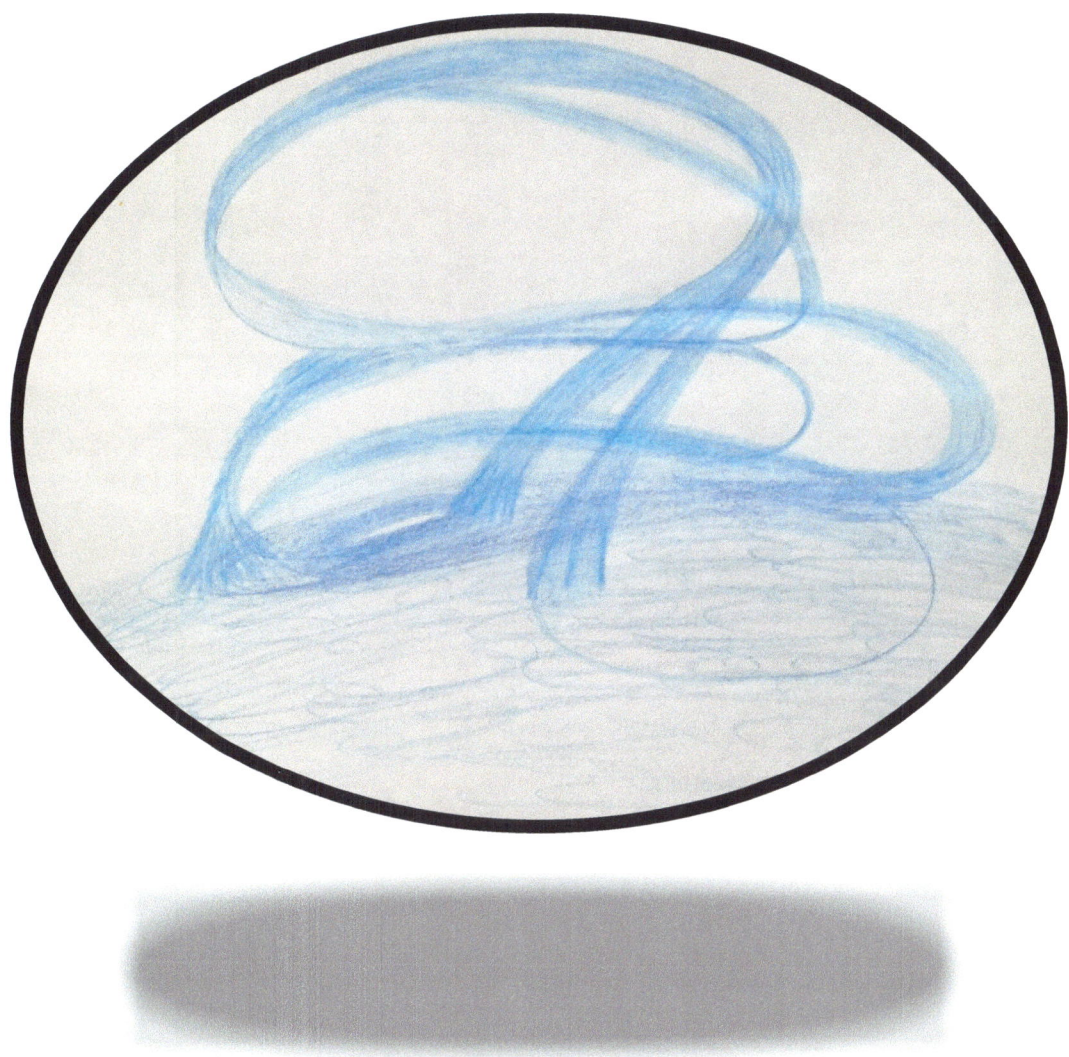

Something reminds me of a beached whale.

On the roads back to NJ... Clinton CT. I didn't even know where I was. I had to look at the receipt to see the address. I had stopped to eat. I do still like their cheeseburgers. I forgot to ask for extra pickles. I sat down alone and looked to my left. There was the picture of the falls. Of course. The staff was too busy to ask if they knew which falls they were. It would be funny if they were upstate NY falls. Can someone ask Mr. McDonald which waterfalls are in the photograph in his store and let me know? I was in store #516 according to the receipt. Oh. Please let him know his employees are doing a good job. They smiled at me. More than once...

The following weekend I went back for the pickup trip. That night I was bombarded with more dreams…

She drove right into the pickup truck they were saying...or right into the boat. I am not sure which. Perhaps she was drunk coming home that night and ran her car into another vehicle…

Then there was a dream of the little league game. The boys were around eight or nine. The first boy got up to bat. The pitcher was really bad. The ball kept bouncing in the dirt on its way in. The count got to full count. The pitch came in… He thought it was another ball. It looked outside the plate. He didn't swing. They called him out on a strike. I don't know if there was an umpire or if someone else was deciding the pitches. The boy laid down on his back in the grass to the side. He didn't go back to the bench. The other team threw the ball around and then the game went on. The other kids on the team were getting hits and getting on base. The boy in the grass was thinking that when he got up again he was going to bat right-handed instead of left-handed…

The breast exam. A woman was lying down and they were doing the exam with a device I have never seen. The nurse was holding it in her hand. An enlarged gland on the right side she said and I think something else. When the exam was done the nurse said she was going to have two women who had similar things to come in and talk with her. Well, I do still have to go to my annual exam so this one may just be for me. A reminder to all of us to go…

The little league game. My brother and I were on the same team when we were kids. Boys and girls could be on the same team. He was a pitcher. His throws were really wild sometimes. Going in the dirt. He only batted one way I think. As far as I can remember. There were other kids who could bat both ways. I always thought it was neat. A talent. Why is this story in here? The boy was ashamed to go back with the team. Called out with the bat sitting on his shoulders. I used to think that was worse than swinging and missing, but now I actually think it's not. He didn't swing because he thought it was a ball. He made a decision based on his judgment. In this case, somebody else said his judgment was off and the game went on. Just like life…we make decisions based on what we know. If someone says that is wrong, well regardless, the game…life goes on. The little boy laid there in the grass…perhaps he was looking up at the clouds…perhaps he was talking to God. He decided he would try the other way…bat write-handed… He had a new strategy. Would his judgment be better from the other side…

When the game is over, everyone shakes hands…good game they say to each other. The pressure off. The winners happy and the losers not so happy. Perhaps his judgment would be better from the other side…is that what they are saying…simply find a way to look at things differently…and maybe the out will become a hit…

The little boy didn't go back with the rest of the team right away. He stayed off to the side in the grass. I don't think it was just because he was ashamed he had been called out. He knew to remove himself. He needed to think. So wise for such a young boy. I wonder who he is…

We had gone to the beach before driving back home. I was sitting there and before I knew it, was drawing in the sand. I used the seashells to see what it was…

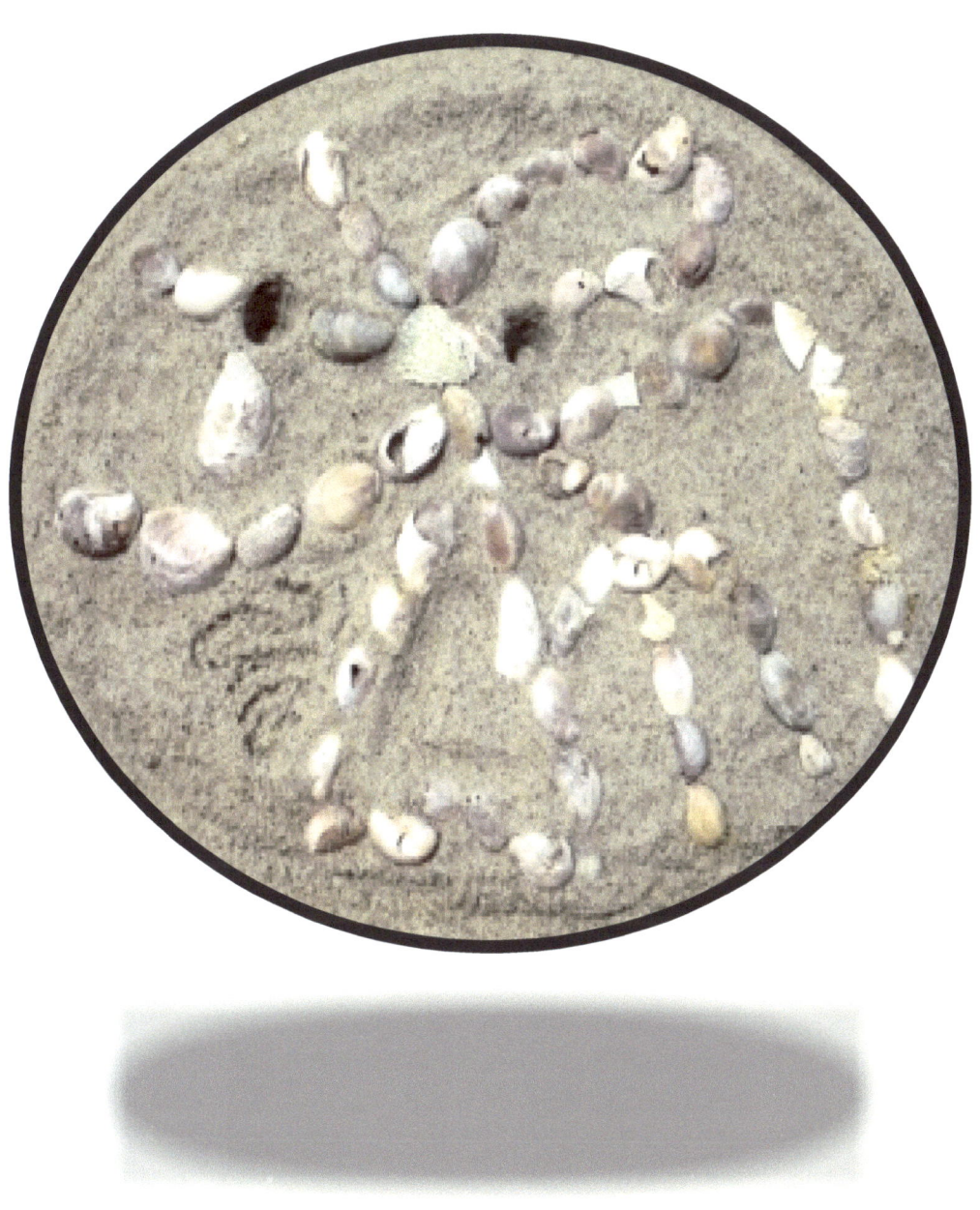

It is the sea monster. He is sad. He has a big tear coming from his left eye. The air was so fresh smelling and the water was so blue at the cape, I couldn't understand why the sea MONSTER was sad. Oh. Is he sad to be called a monster? It is not his fault he is scary and mean looking. That is the way he was made. Oh. When we figure out how to bat the other way…can we also figure out how to look the other way…to see the beauty in the ugly?

The lovely in the monster…

Dedicated to Gail...for caring and sharing

About the Author and *Illustrator*

RL Lane has published the EcarreT series and a collection of short story art books featuring the author's illustrations. The EcarreT series begins with "Chapel Street Signs"…

…unexplained connections that challenge us to beli ve. A woman, a Dad a Doctor, a cat and mouse, a horse and tale tell their stories. "Do you beli ve in spirits?" I asked my friend. "Well look", he said, "I believe there are things that cannot be explained..." Oh. Plus, hear ov a Mom's battle with her struggle to connect to the woman...her little girl.

Welcome to EcarreT...a world
Where everyone cares
Why did I have to create it in...

A fiction fantasy world?

You may already know why, but you will see regardless of what you believe as a girl's journey of love and faith on her "Touring Machine" take her on the best journey of her mundane life. A life well on its way takes a turn in a direction that could've never been seen or even dreamed...

The author can be contacted at:

RosaLeeeLane@gmail.com
www.Amazon.com/author/readrllane

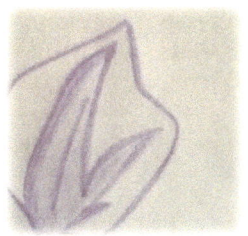

ISBN: 1515215911
ISBN-13: 978-1515215912

www.ingramcontent.com/pod-product-compliance
Lightning Source LLC
Chambersburg PA
CBHW050433180526
45159CB00006B/2518